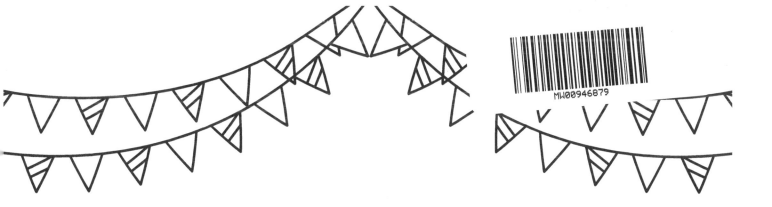

This book belongs to:

_____

I chose the country_____

for the following holiday _____.

Color the flag in the colors of your chosen country

Where in the world?

Put an arrow where your chosen
country is located.

The country _____ is located on

the _____continent.

I chose the holiday _____.

I think this holiday is interesting because_____
_____

Dates of holiday: _____

Which people celebrate? (everyone in the country, a certain group/organization)
_____

_____

Summarize the history of the holiday:

_____

_____

_____

_____

Websites and Books Used for Information

Holidays Festivals and Traditions

List the festivals, traditional clothing, and routines associated with the holiday. There are additional places within this book to go into further detail.

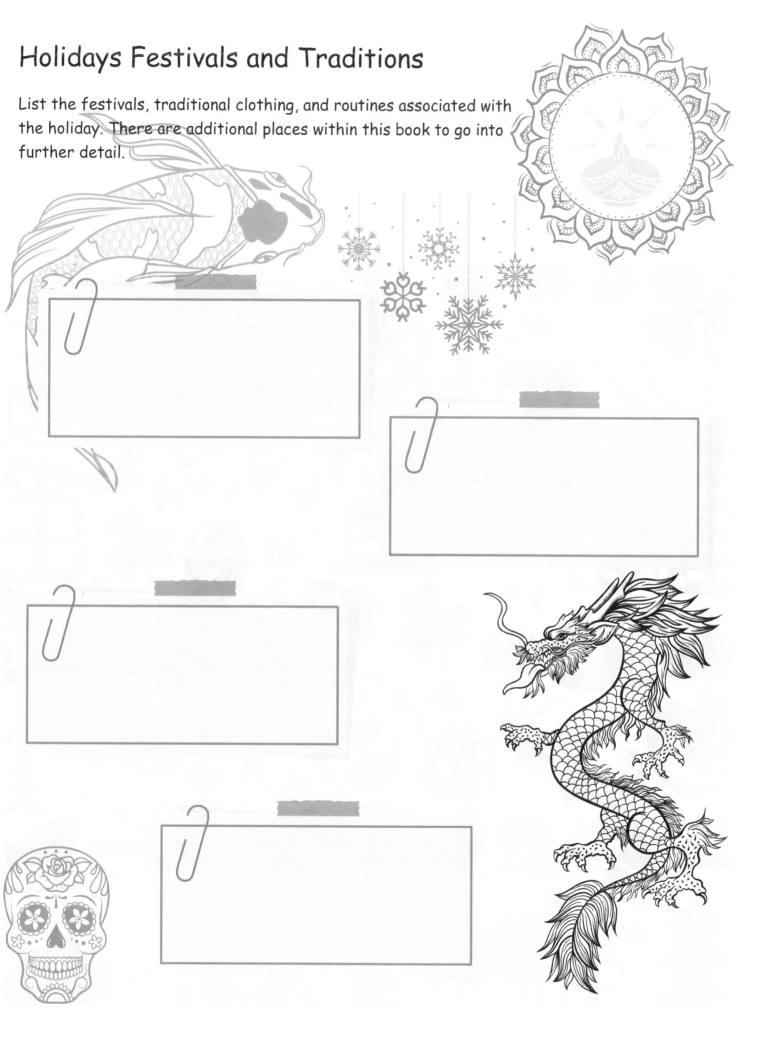

Using inspiration from either the country's flag or colors associated with the holiday, decorate the gift box.

Holiday Scavenger Hunt

Collect or draw the items you find either online or around the house related to the holiday

- Red
- Green
- Fuzzy
- Smooth
- Shiny
- Festive
- Food
- Unique
- Yellow
- Small

The city is hosting a festival and fireworks. Help your friends navigate the streets to find the festivities.

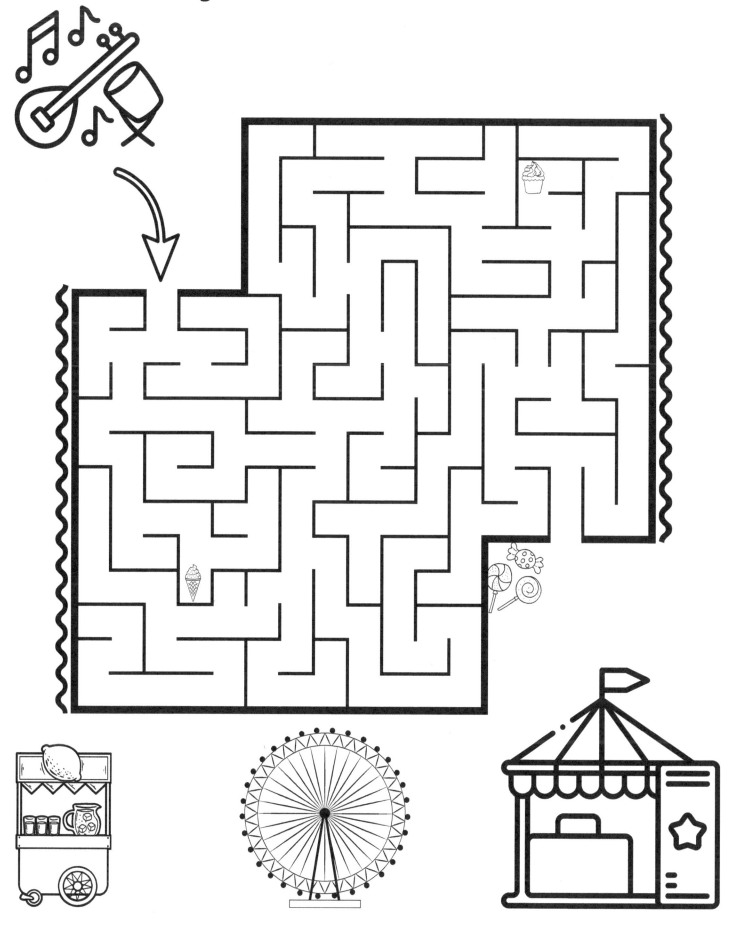

You made it!
Put a star next to the activity you
want to try first.

Word Search

```
A  X  C  F  T  U  I  K  L  A  D  I  K  W  Q
E  R  F  T  L  D  A  U  O  P  Q  W  D  X  C
M  H  O  L  I  D  A  Y  C  V  B  N  E  A  S
H  F  O  Y  U  K  B  V  G  H  V  N  C  M  X
U  N  D  I  M  W  A  D  V  M  G  H  O  U  T
N  C  I  Q  N  K  S  O  C  U  J  Z  R  A  C
Q  O  I  G  L  I  H  T  S  P  W  A  T  Y
V  S  D  R  I  N  K  S  U  I  W  N  T  D  K
E  T  R  T  Y  O  D  F  G  C  N  M  I  U  O
C  U  W  S  T  H  H  K  L  I  T  V  O  X  Q
B  M  D  M  Q  A  S  X  W  Z  C  L  N  E  Q
F  E  F  E  S  T  I  V  A  L  P  Q  S  W  X
H  S  M  I  C  S  G  K  O  C  E  B  W  T  C
Z  D  U  K  I  G  H  P  W  C  R  A  F  T  S
J  U  P  Z  Y  N  Q  I  S  N  I  O  N  Q  E
```

HOLIDAY
FOOD
LIGHTS

DECORATIONS
DRINKS
MUSIC
FESTIVAL

CRAFTS
COSTUMES
HATS

Find the Hidden Items

Mask   Apple

Drum   Calendar

Mug   Clock

Dancer   Candle

Gift   Flower

You and your friends are chosen to help decorate for the festivities. Add decorations around the room that best represent the holiday from your research.

Don't forget to about food and music!

Make it brighter!

Many holidays use light as part of a ceremony or to make it festive. Draw the lights associated with the holiday. If there aren't any lights specific to your chosen holiday, color the lights below in the colors associated with the holiday.

Mystery Message

Example:

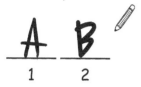

A   B
‾   ‾
1   2

Fill in the letters in order and use it to
decode the mystery message.

‾‾ ‾‾ ‾‾ ‾‾ ‾‾ ‾‾ ‾‾ ‾‾ ‾‾ ‾‾
1   2   3   4   5   6   7   8   9   10

‾‾ ‾‾ ‾‾ ‾‾ ‾‾ ‾‾ ‾‾ ‾‾ ‾‾ ‾‾
11   12   13   14   15   16   17   18   19   20

‾‾ ‾‾ ‾‾ ‾‾ ‾‾ ‾‾
21   22   23   24   25   26

Mystery Message

‾‾ ‾‾ ‾‾ ‾‾ ‾‾ ‾‾   ‾‾ ‾‾ ‾‾
20   18   25   9   14   7   14   5   23

‾‾ ‾‾ ‾‾ ‾‾ ‾‾ ‾‾   ‾‾ ‾‾ ‾‾
20   8   9   14   7   19   3   1   14

‾‾ ‾‾ ‾‾ ‾‾ ‾‾ ‾‾ ‾‾ ‾‾ ‾‾ ‾‾ ‾‾ ‾‾
2   18   9   14   7   22   1   18   9   5   20   25

‾‾ ‾‾ ‾‾   ‾‾ ‾‾ ‾‾ ‾‾ ‾‾ ‾‾ ‾‾ ‾‾
1   14   4   5   24   3   9   20   5   13   5   20

‾‾ ‾‾ ‾‾ ‾‾   ‾‾ ‾‾ ‾‾ ‾‾   ‾‾ ‾‾ ‾‾ ‾‾ •
9   14   20   15   25   15   21   18   12   9   6   5

People like to take pictures during holiday festivities.
Draw a picture of a photo you would take if you were there.

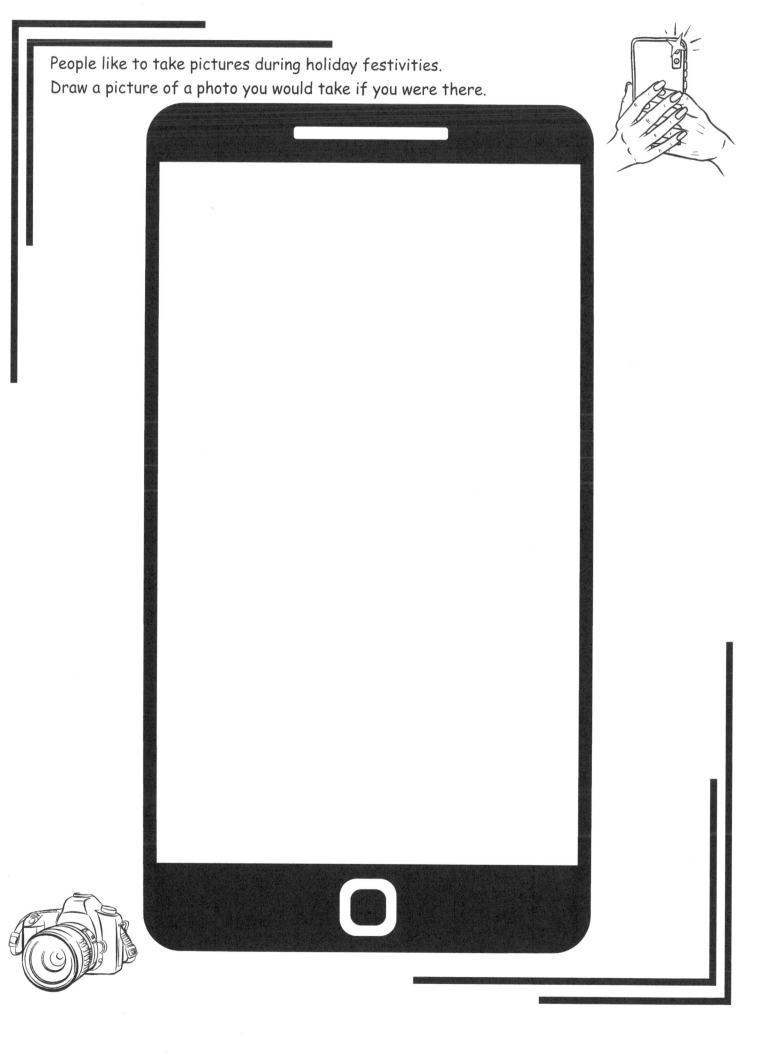

Plants

Write or draw plants traditional to the country's holiday

Music and books related to the holiday
Put a star next to your favorite

Typical Holiday Food and Drinks

MENU

Using your research, create a menu for a holiday event.
Add the recipes to the following pages.

Appetizers

———————————————————

———————————————————

———————————————————

Main Dishes

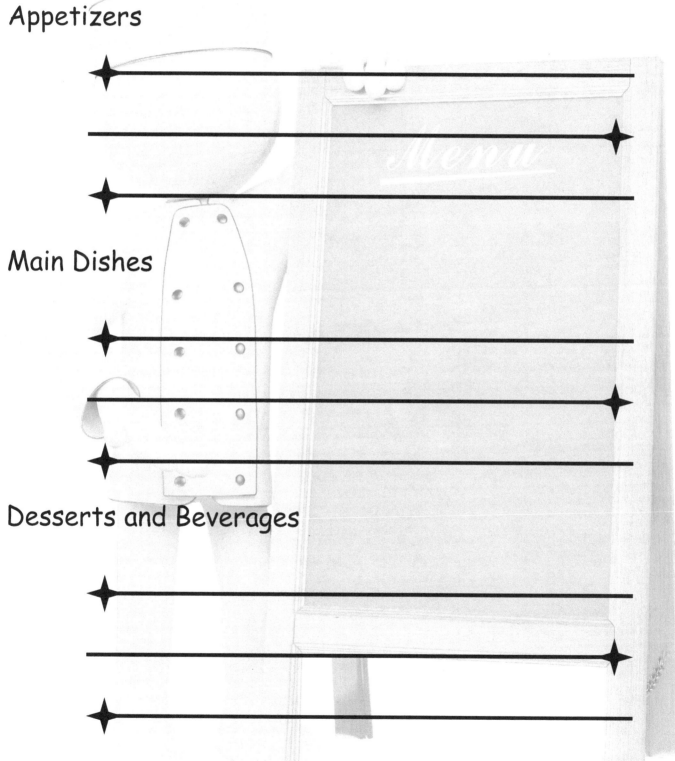

———————————————————

———————————————————

———————————————————

Desserts and Beverages

———————————————————

———————————————————

———————————————————

Recipe #1 _____

Prep Time: _____

Total Time: _____

Notes: _____

Ingredients: _____

_____

_____

_____

_____

_____

Instructions: _____

_____

_____

_____

_____

_____

_____

_____

_____

_____

_____

Recipe #2 _____

Prep Time: _____

Total Time: _____

Kitchen

Notes: _____

Ingredients: _____

_____

_____

_____

_____

_____

Instructions: _____

_____

_____

_____

_____

_____

_____

_____

_____

JAM

cook book

Recipe #3 _____   Prep Time: _____
                                        Total Time: _____

Notes: _____

Ingredients: _____

_____

_____

_____

_____

_____

Instructions: _____

_____

_____

_____

_____

_____

_____

_____

_____

_____

_____

Recipe #4 _____

Prep Time: _____
Total Time: _____

Notes: _____

Ingredients: _____

_____

_____

_____

_____

_____

Instructions: _____

_____

_____

_____

_____

_____

_____

_____

_____

_____

_____

_____

_____

Recipe #5 _____

Prep Time: _____
Total Time: _____

Notes: _____

Ingredients: _____

_____

_____

_____

_____

_____

_____

Instructions: _____

_____

_____

_____

_____

_____

_____

_____

_____

_____

_____

_____

Recipe #6 _____   Prep Time: _____

Total Time: _____

Notes: _____

Ingredients: _____

_____

_____

_____

_____

_____

Instructions: _____

_____

_____

_____

_____

_____

_____

_____

_____

_____

_____

_____

_____

Recipe #7 _____

Prep Time: _____

Total Time: _____

Notes: _____

Ingredients: _____

_____

_____

_____

_____

_____

_____

Instructions: _____

_____

_____

_____

_____

_____

_____

_____

_____

_____

_____

_____

Recipe #8 _____   Prep Time: _____

                                              Total Time: _____

Notes: _____

Ingredients: _____

_____

_____

_____

_____

_____

_____

Instructions: _____

_____

_____

_____

_____

_____

_____

_____

_____

_____

_____

Recipe #9 _____

Prep Time: _____

Total Time: _____

Notes: _____

Ingredients: _____

Instructions: _____

Story Telling/Journal Page

Hints: Would you like to travel to the country to participate
in the festivities?
What are your favorite things about the traditions?
Did you try any of the recipes?

Story Telling/Journal Page #2

Made in United States
Troutdale, OR
12/07/2024

25899821R10033